Their Lives...

Still Matter...

Part 1 of:
"One Last Cheer."

DEATH of a Linden Cheerleader...

"MURDER STILL UNSOLVED FIVE YEARS LATER."

&

Women **also found murdered close to the owner's parents** other residence. She recently discussed it with her folks,

who had **no clue themselves about such a person lurking in their area. AUTHOR** has family who own a home in such area, such alleged serial killer lurks in such a wonderful community.

Til' he was finally caught,and at least for "1"victim,brought to justice for which we are praying ALL of these victims receive their justice as the family has long-awaited,,for far too many years…"

Author:

Women 4 Justice Publishing N.Y.C.

POWERHOUSE WOMEN CONSULTING, MOTIVATIONAL EMPOWERMENT GROUP.

Redhead Beach-house Productions N.Y.C.

Redhead Bella Magazine...

Copyright Protection
**ALL RIGHTS RESERVED
2017-2020...**

Tips/Helpline/Leads/private anonymous information et.al.,

To speak directly with the author or her virtual e-staff 24hrs.a day: 1-855-BELLA17

Cannot get through,no answer?

Then call our other help/hotline and or for those who are also fighting for their civil rights et.al., and or suing for such involving one's constitutional + civil rights involving an injustice et.al.,

1-929-277-7848(for those who are in violation of their civil rights pro-se litigants et.al.,) and or those who have a tip and or a lead involving the death of the victim, AMBER DUNCAN WILSON and or any other featured in our book(s) thank you...."

PREFACE (1)

EVERY LIFE SHOULD MATTER,

WHEN AN INNOCENT LIFE NOW IN HEAVEN RESTING IN PEACE TOO SOON.

ALL *BECAUSE OF ONE NEFARIOUS SOUL WHO NEED TO BE CAUGHT, TRIED...*

CONVICTED.

SENT TO DEATH ROW.

LIVIN' comfortably in a prison cell is NOT true JUSTICE.

Our Author is dedicating this book to them, simply because **their life...**

#STILL Matter ...

"Facts et.al. taken from all news reports, local/cable news and newspapers on the senseless murder of those cited and or the missing et.al., May God bless us all, and our families and my justice come for such victims + the missing return to their loved ones, soon ..."

Chapter I

"From Graduating from Linden H.S., Class of 2012..

Weeks later, a short trip to the neighboring

Dunkin Donuts on

N.Wood Avenue,

to RIP senselessly,

by a punk, coward with a gun..."

She cheered her last game.

(Photo's courtesy of NBC Television News Network, New York)

Next, during such year of her last cheer?

Her Linden H.S. Prom, followed in 2012 by her High School Graduation. . .

I, as many parents, would remember going to my daughter's graduation, as my daughter, was about the same age as Amber, couple years young,

and how proud I was to be her mother, seeing my own daughter graduate from high school.

This had to be one of Amber Duncan-Wilson most happiest days of her life, to be graduating from Linden High School.

Just a few weeks later. . . Her life sadly abruptly changed forever, as her loving family and friends, all who knew and cared and love Amber..

A local stop at a Dunkin Donuts, the author frequent, in town known as **NORTH WOOD AVENUE right across the street from the town's busy 7-Eleven. This area I am always feeling so secure in, when I am driving/walking in such area, of N.WOOD AVENUE ...**

Low-crime residential quiet area of Linden, New Jersey, in Union County.

MURDER is non-existent/quite rare.

During such time, four to five years ago from time of book publication,

the beautiful town of Linden, had ZERO...(not 1 murder)as records show ergo, makin'it a low-crime area, with nice homes, nestled on a tree lined street just like the author's residence.

The author residence was only a few blocks at the time away from the victim for whom this much warranted book, is dedicated to, as other unsolved murder(s)for women of color, black and hispanic brown, who are either missing, and or later found murdered." All victims matter yes. However, we are dedicating this book to 1 imparticular. The author's neighbor, in a town that he loved, as the author so much. Such victim deserve JUSTICE. So far, she has received none, nor her loving father, and her entire family. It's long overdue. The area is a joyous one, in town. Diversity is clear. 1 moment in time, in Linden, has changed that, forever."

Linden is 1 of those town's that many attempt to move to."

From the local Ice Cream parlor, to Domino's, Linden Shopping Mall to the train station,to the nearby police dept.,on North Wood,beautiful parks, and an in-town lovely movie theatre and local lovely library.

Author

loved raising her 2 daughters in such time,where she knew as herself they all would be safe, since she carried her daughter's in the womb…" I always knew LINDEN was 1 of the best safest residential towns to raise a family,to live for years on end,in our U.S.A.

Author daughter's also enjoyed and loved the city(still do)of Linden,just like their mom."

Linden, NJ has lovely homes and new condo's in the center of town, right on North Wood. "Great schools & neighbors…"

House of worship throughout town…

Lovely parks close by for the kids and families to attend during warm/nice summer days, to enjoy and all local shops throughout, with minimal to no crime. Sadly…1 summer's night, the town changed forever…

1 night…

"A TRIP ON NORTH WOOD changed all of that along with a local family whose life is now changed, forever, in the beautiful low-crime, wonderful **suburban residential town of LINDEN…"**

#NEVER2FORGETAMBER …

She loved her family...
She loved her friends, who loved her back...

She loved cheering our Linden High School sports teams, for years, proudly.

She loved cheerleading/dancin' and was so astute, prudent smart teen-child, who was just graduating from L.H.S., in Linden.

She had a loving father, step-mother and family who loved and adored her, and extended family and "real" friends, who respect miss and truly love her.

She, and her life mattered, and **still do.**

She has a name ...

Her name is ...#AMBERWilsonDuncan and her life matters.
When a woman cannot walk from her Dunkin Donuts back home with her friend, her life is cut short on a busy residential shoppin' area low crime WOOD) and is gunned down, before midnight, by an animal and yet her killer is still free to terrorize other good American souls, there is a problem. A MAJOR problem. This is wrong on so many levels, and we pray meanwhile as always for her family, awaiting our community & the family delayed JUSTICE.

CHAPTER II

"The delay..."

So many queries/questions…

So much time has now passed, but yet, to us who are caring/and following her Amber's short life story,tragic ending we care and we are all awaiting JUSTICE for her as it is taking way too long when you are having her KILLER out in the street, eating, relaxing, not at all feeling remorse for taking her life,

a young life promised,and now gone,yet her killin' is still marked as a cold-case and it's not right.Amber was murdered.Ergo, she clearly deserves the same exact attention as other victims are receiving/and or have received prior to her early demise.Many feel she is not getting it.Amber is still on the minds of mine, of many and encompassing her former neighbor… The author …

HER LIFE, still matters and more media focus has to be exerted involving the senseless murder of one of Linden,NJ most promising students,graduate and someone's loving daughter,for which this good loving father deserve justice for his child,gunned down, on her way home from a local eatery.

Women 4 Justice Publishing and RedheadBellaMagazine today are writing this book in memory of AMBER and so many others in the NEW JERSEY DELAWARE PA,(tri-state)and tri-state area,cited in our book,and or on our facebook/and or website(s) to missing black and Hispanic Latina girls, under 18 in our nation capital(Washington D.C.) and down south off I-95 North Carolina, where an alleged serial-killer also lurked for years!(No one knew a serial killer lurked right in a nice rural quiet NC low crime town)and other killings that should have not happened, ever." But it did happen, and we are here to say that just because their lives are cut short,

their lives still matter, and they deserve JUSTICE, along with more news coverage on their untimely death to get the word up and KEEP the pressure on such so we can get these deaths,resolved,for which the victims are rip but their family members,are still here crying, mourning, shocked,hurt and deserve such **FINAL** justice per victim, encompassing any woman who yes may have had a drug issue,worked the streets, but their lives still matter, and you have some who were just going to a store, or shopping,or at a dunkin donuts, or as in Delaware, was working at a sneaker store, and she and her co-worker were found dead.

Who would do this to 2 innocent good souls working, trying to simply make a living, didn't hurt anyone in life, but yet were robbed of their bright future,and yet no accountability,no arrest.

Where is the media on the victim murder?

TWO innocent victims,in Delaware,RIP far too soon,yet no media. No arrest. No justice.We pray their justice is visible soon.

Why has this monster not been caught yet?

We shall delve into this,

and also leave a help/hotline # for those who might just have a lead, a tip and forward it to such authorities, who are covering **from AMBER's brutal murder, to the victims (2) in a store in DELAWARE**, 1 state over from NJ where other lives also cut short, all deserve justice and the victim's families. God bless us all. We thank you for reading and for your support.

CHAPTER III

FREEDOM IS SO VALUABLE/WE ALL

DESERVE TO LIVE a LONG HEALTHY BLESSED PRODUCTIVE LIFE...

To have a decent nice good god blissful life,not to be shot

dead by our own people,or shot dead by anyone...

Authorites appeal to the public,and our community,for all, with information to simply pick up the phone,and or even text a tip msg., et.al., to the Union County Police Dept., and or NJ STATE POLICE and or most relevant, reach directly (where AMBER's murder took place) reach the city directly and the lead investigators on the case, Detective Travis Koziol at (908) 474-8500 or contact Detective Andrew Dellaquila of the county homicide task force at (908) 527-4500.

Also, you're able to contact the Union County,New Jersey "Crimestopper"hotline @ (908) 654-TIPS (8477) THERE IS A REWARD.

When a person is buying tea,or coffee or a donut at the local Dunkin Donuts,

in a quiet nice suburban blue-collar town,residential area, an hour or two before midnight, who just graduated school and was on her way to becoming something spectacular in life,

had a loving father around/family and friends who truly love and care for such a person,then suddenly, a bullet (intentionally)takes such a promising

GOOD person's life, people are within such right to… DEMAND SWIFT JUSTICE. FIVE YEARS IS NOT SWIFT. What is going on? When will justice come for this innocent girl?

For more on this senseless death where thousand or more showed how much they cared by arriving at her funeral, visit the link directed below.

http://www.nj.com/news/index.ssf/2012/07/funeral_held_for_linden_teen_k.html

"We release such book during the 5th year of Amber's anniversary of her murder.

The animal who killed her, is still livin' a free life.

He needs to be arrested, indicted, and finally brought to justice."

(908)474-8500
(Report whatever tip you have, no matter how miniscule.) It might lead the police/detectives et.al., in Linden, NJ to finally procure a big break! AMBER DUNCAN WILSON deserve justice!

#RIP Amber Duncan-Wilson…Such book warranted, is clearly dedicated to you, in our Author's community she has always loved, suburban residential community, low-crime area, great caring neighbors, wonderful people who truly care. If everyone simply would just share what they know, if only 1 good soul release information on the murder of such a beloved daughter and student, and community teen-child of Linden, NJ this murder would be solved." I pray for her. We all do, for her eternal peace as we continue, the community to fight for what is right and that is to bring more attention, to remain cognitive in our beloved community, and demand such FINAL long-awaited justice for our neighbor:

Amber Duncan Wilson, and also other nearby local/state communities near, and **up and down I-95** for such lives,albeit,yes cut short,but their lives all **still** matter."

Until there are **VIDEO-CAM(s)literally** on EACH and EVERY block, of our lovely communities, also in the projects/hood area(s) from the hood to suburban areas, camera's on EACH block, to catch a potential crime in progress,et.al., you're to speak up! This girl was brutally murdered.She did not deserve it,and worse as she is RIP,the ANIMAL who snuffed her life away from her is still roaming our streets, free to still live his life.

Many concerned citizens,out of state and in state we have spoken to at time of facilitating our book(s) are outraged/want justice for amber the cheerleader,who was gunned down."

Many blame the Police Dept., for not providing enough manpower to search for dear sweet Amber Duncan Wilson.

Our research,consulting WOMEN 4 JUSTICE PUBLISHING NYC and our AUTHOR do not blame such police. We are sure they are doing what they can,for which we are simply praying day after day, the police will soon be making an arrest.

For myself:

I keep praying to mi self each day when drive by in linden,nj her old residence/the family area in which she resided in,and loved.

"I, at times still(five years later) ride by the area

where AMBER DUNCAN-WILSON lost her life so needlessly,so senselessly, and I say a prayer, in hopes her killer will finally be caught soon.

The author tears simply have not cease, and will not til'

justice has surfaced for AMBER DUNCAN-WILSON.

The former MAYOR of LINDEN,NJ publicly told the press: The "1" case he regret was not solved under and during his long tenure was of the cheerleader/the great student at LHS, sweet, Amber Duncan Wilson. He publicly stated such. I hope(and will be contacting as a concerned and dedicated citizen/civil rights advocate and take ACTION activist, who truly care about what is going on in our suburban residential community and other communities, I will be reaching again the MAYOR(new) Derek Armstead. I pray more media coverage will arise, to keep the now dim-spotlight on a murder that 1 expert I've interviewed, was citing how this case is surely not unsolvable but has to be a center-focus,and not "pushed back into the file drawer."

 Many, as cited earlier, have been blaming the department, and continually for years online as well, by saying they are yes, supposed to be properly aggressively investigating such victim shooting and yet, here we are approaching the 5th **year of Amber's senseless death 2 or a few weeks after** she blessfully and happily became a LINDEN HIGH SCHOOL **GRADUATE making her family so proud.**

But yet there is no one in custody?

You're turning on the media, and the news coverage is now basically non-existent. Now why is that…"

Why isn't AMBER's story and brutal early death on the news today? Yesterday? Two nights ago? On her 2nd anniversary? Third…or 4th or 5th…

This is now to some a cold-case,that will never be solved, but author feel in her astute mind,and her kind beautiful heart it will be,if more tips,and more media first and foremost,remain on the case.

When i turn on the news, and or look online news at NJ biggest newspaper, the Star-Ledger/NJ Advance Media,

i do not see any update on either an arrest of the punk-coward, killer with a gun who took such her life so soon, without reason of such validity, and i do not hear anything insofar as any **new leads.**

Why are there no new leads/public info on the death of Amber?

She deserve JUSTICE.

This murder involving the happy,good spirited,smart, wonderful Linden **teenager has gone cold,and this is just simply INEXCUSABLE.**

The victim father, who loves his daughter so much, is now force to live with the fact the murderer is somewhere, feasibly, most likely **NOT** in our beloved town in nice LINDEN and or nearby,in the more "hood" areas not far from nice quiet low-crime area of Linden,feasibly in Newark,or another hood hanging with his "boys."

He is just "free after committing such a brutal homicide."

Simply just living as if he has not a care in the world!This man need to be arrested and caught,as it is have been five years but yet feel like it is back in 2012.

We release the book on and or around the day,year of Amber's brutal murder,

because the author is very fond of her Linden area, and she thinks of this case almost as much as she breathes … That is how much the author is praying the killer is found/more news coverage is needed as a higher REWARD as in other cases so we can catch the suspect, who took a promising young linden,nj life away for no reason whatsoever.

WE PRAY SO MUCH FOR YOUR FATHER,

STEP-MOTHER,AND FAMILY,AMBER …"

Photo (courtesy of NBC-News 4) in NYC. #RIP

Amber Duncan-Wilson . . .

You're not forgotten by the author.

Such crimes that go unsolved leave a hole in one's heart,for which the victims, no matter what they were doing at the time of such demise, such early trip to heaven now rip, they did not deserve whatsoever what happen to them,and in this book,we focus on THEM because their lives ...#STILL matter.

From the time of such books published **by the author, just about 11,106** black souls have been murdered viciously by other blacks, most recent statistics demonstrate everyone, and this number reportedly is much higher today." Sadly, this has now happened to a linden,nj resident,and she deserve justice.AMBER DUNCAN WILSON DESERVE JUSTICE.**WHERE** IS HER JUSTICE?

There is **no excuse** to take a life of your own kind, your own people, and or any life,of such innocent person and or persons. When such death happens, in such manner, justice is DEMANDED, and must come swift.

Photo of Amber Wilson,courtesy of the NJ biggest newspaper ; The Star-Ledger News now refer to as NJ.com(Advanced Media) Michael Henn, supervisor of the Union County Homicide Task Force.Such supervisor cited years ago how,more people might know about this crime. Other reporters, and others cite how cite that Amber feasibly knew, her killer.

Amber had so much promised in the quiet low-crime area of suburban residential nice Linden,NJ. Her future dreams died sadly forever, when her life was cut short the evening of and shortly before the midnight hour of JULY 9th 2012. I personally love Linden,NJ and I know this much.If this was my daughter I would want JUSTICE/DEMAND IT and EXPECT JUSTICE.

It has been 5 years now, and AMBER killing still remain unsolved.WHERE IS THE MEDIA ON AMBER KILLING?

KILLER REMAIN FREE to harm again.

To eat,sleep just fine and to do what he has been doing, living his abhorrent life day,day out.

He must be caught.Simple as that.**SIMPLE AS THAT.**

If you have any tips/leads no matter how miniscule reach

AUTHOR directly.

She will forward such anonymous information to the police immediate,lead detective on case and or leave on her public social media popular news feeds; pages,as all links will be shared below,or at the conclusion of her book.

Thank you. #AMBERDUNCANWILSON

#JUSTICE4AmberDuncanWilson

The Linden Police Dept. and the Union County Prosecutor office,reported that Amber and her friend(name never released) were both walking home from the local area Dunkin Donuts,east of North Wood Avenue;(turning onto Hussa Street,in the area, where reportedly another friend lived and Amber's family.

She never quite made it.

Amber, age 18 years young, was brutally gunned down,by such gunman after she was "robbed." Another suburban residential town of RAHWAY (minutes from the Linden area) comes into play where such detective located a cell phone belonging the victims

Flagrantly, the killer(still not caught)discards the phone, and remains on the run, living his life while poor Amber is in heaven, far too soon.

"This man has to be caught, because another year,another week,day month he is not behind bars, the family and those who love her will never quite have full justice... #AmberDuncanLife still matter. Simple as that. Just like all them "other victims,not black or brown,Hispanic, et.al., and yet they are also receiving more news coverage,and we hope that AMBER story will reach other news outlets,and nationwide statewide,news channels & cable news to 48hours, to 20/20 HLN,CNN,MSNBC,all others news outlets, just like other cases have received, AMBER, whether black,Hispanic,white, or Asian,indian et.al such life matter and she deserve justice,as her family."

Five years,and the killer still is not behind bars...We pray that justice for Amber shall be visible soon.

#RIPAmber

You're remembered each minute of the day Amber,

as others featured in this new book under WOMEN 4 JUSTICE Publishing where we focus on such victims who all share 1 thing in common and that is the fact the Black and the Brown listed,throughout such book, are still receiving **NO JUSTICE.**

It is like they were killed, without any fault of their own, and yet,

 JUSTICE isn't feasibly relevant to those in charge of conducting a full-scale AGGRESSIVE investigatory into per victim, who deserve just that, and the loving family members they have left behind." The lives lost, through such violence, are LIVES that #still matter.

-Chapter IV-

In the tri-state area of PA.NJ.,DE.,we have lost additionally 2 other innocent victims over a decade ago, as their future's were stolen from them, within a blink of an eye…

WHERE is the killer and when will JUSTICE be served?

#PRAYING4JUSTICEinDELAWARE

It has been about 13 years now, when a woman, (South of where Amber Wilson-Duncan in Linden NJ(Northern NJ) these two victims in DELAWARE still have not received justice. <u>**Another**</u> **victim(2)one male/female, both innocent.**

One of them are not too much older than Amber Wilson-Duncan,in North Jersey & the other was same age(18.)In the neighboring state of **DELAWARE, another** woman, working @

Delaware's Casual Male Big & Tall Store …

Both were closing up,shift was ending.

Both were heading home after work where they would have been clearly safe,and out of such gunman's way,who had no regard for a human life, that both should be alive and with us in our communities today and with such loving family,and all who cared and loved them,but they are not.

Still…

after a decade and a few years, at time of such book published, Jessica and her co-worker only 18 years young,

Matthew Macerato were both murdered, in an execution style homicide. It was cruel…senseless,

and justice is long overdue.

This is taking way too long, as local Delaware/NJ tri-state area citizens, PA.,(no arrest since early mid 2000s.)

I feel the loving mother's pain, both of the Delaware mothers, who lost their children so quickly, in the most violent way. These 2 lives from our tri-state matter...

We will continue to follow this story, **until** God calls us home, til' we are old and grey, to see if JUSTICE for such innocent victims in Delaware is seen, as well as for all others who still have not gotten justice, nor their heartbreaking families.

Even though the killer is not yet behind bars or on death row where belongs, we shall continue to keep this book circulating on social media, and our page up in support of JUSTICE for the lives cited in our books, because these lives #still matter,even while they are resting in peace.

(Family Photo,made available to the public and DelawareNewsOnline,courtesy of the Watson Family.) 13 yrs, as of 2017 still…NO JUSTICE for JESSIC. No justice for her innocent hard-working co-worker."

. (Photo made available/ courtesy of Matt's family)and DelawareNewsOnline.com ...

These two deserve justice.A shocking murder has taken place and yet NEITHER one, innocent victims families are receiving justice..Such case deserve MORE MEDIA COVERAGE,same as other specific-cases receive,on all news channels,regularly.Sad to say,this is not the case.

We remember you both,and we pray JUSTICE shall be served soon.#RIP **Jessica** life **still matter as** Matt's and we are all praying for JUSTICE soon to be served,and not to keep this case,a cold case,because their lives ..#STILL matter and I think of you often from when I first learned of this brutal crime in my tri-state area Jessica Watson and Matt, as your child(Jessica) being forced to grow up,live her life without you.

May justice come soon for yourself and matt,and your familia.

GOD BLESS US ALL.

-Chapter V-

SOUTH JERSEY(minutes from Philly,PA and Delaware) In South Jersey.

The murder of Juan Cuevas was tragic. So un-necessary.

Mr.Cuevas, age 36 years old was found dead,

lying on the bed inside of his home,back in mid upper 2000's...(2006)

He owned his own business at the time called GI June's Auto Parts in Philadelphia, and the killer still has not been arrested.

Children were inside of Juan's home at the time, and they were forcibly bound, and placed in an upstairs bedroom, and also in the bathroom, as Mr.Cuevas wife, Wilma, was however not home, and was reportedly at work during such time...

The killer or killers took Mr.Cuevas to the upstairs bedroom, where sadly, his life came to an end,by a vicious beating,by such suspect or suspects.

We pray for his loving wife,the children,now older,and all who are awaiting JUSTICE for Mr.Juan Cuevas... His life #STILL matter.

UPDATE: Recent on 1 of the untimely death(s)of victims featured in our books,and that is the fact that 1 killer is off of the streets, never to harm and or assault or kill another innocent person again.

JUAN CUEVAS's KILLER IS OFF OF THE STREETS, PRAISE GOD.

There was a reward of almost $10,000 for some time to find this killer and bring him to justice, and or for such tips leading to an arrest;and it has paid off.

The killer was arrested.. Let us hope more are arrested as no killer belong on the streets, but in prison and or on DEATH ROW.(THE AUTHOR WHOLLY SUPPORTS DEATH FOR DEATH **when such innocent party is killed at no fault of their own.)**

She <u>does not</u> believe they should be allowed to sit in a cell, eat,watch tv, talk with anyone, have a prison(life)while the victim is **RIP too soon in early predicated** upon one's **cowardly vicious nefarious** act.

She only support such **<u>DEATH ROW</u>** if there is concrete evidence, full-proof,that leaves NO DOUBT insofar as the

person being the actual killer. RIP MR.CUEVAS and our condolences again to your familia.

-Chapter VI-

Tomiene Jones, age 19.

Where is this young mother?Tomiene, deserve justice. This is so sad when you're thinking about another woman has gone missing and yet, NO MEDIA.Not for years.

WHY NOT?

NOT A SHRED OF MEDIA/NEWS,RELATING TO THIS YOUNG LADY. on this woman,same as AMBER DUNCAN WILSON.

Ms.Jones child is a teenager now.I cry just thinking about her daughter and her entire family.They deserve justice. Such victim, resided in South Jersey area, reportedly in Gloucester County, Ms.Tomiene Jones, who should be tonight home with those who love and care and miss her.

Tomiene was age nineteen and reportedly by the press,

was a mother.Ms.Jones had gone missing and at first she was listed as a woman who was missing.(Disappearance investigation.)Then about six months later, in early 2000s it turned into a homicide investigation. We pray one day she will receive justice,as her loving family,because Tomiene Jones life #still matters. Case barely received any *real* media.

IF YOU HAVE ANY INFORMATION ABOUT TOMIENE, PLEASE CONTACT IMMEDIATE:

Missing Persons Unit

Contact the Unit
(609) 882-2000 ext 2554
e-mail: missingp@gw.njsp.org Or simply call 911(reach your local police dept.) because Ms.Jones deserve justice, and so does her family.

-Chapter VII-

SAMANTHA LANG-

Ms.Lang, age twenty-two year old had gone missing.

Ms.Lang, was found with her throat slashed, in the state of **Pennsylvania**.Samantha, as news report cite, had just began working a a new job,during 2004.

 Her killer is still allow to walk the streets, eat, sleep well,without fret, as he still has not been arrested.

We pray for her family and we hope the killer 1 day, is caught... Samantha Lang and her family deserve justice for her,because as she is RIP for years in heaven, her life #STILL matters.

Bonus Chapter:

"Black and Hispanic Latino's missing as media has reported in 2017 at an all time high, back to back, in our nation's capital, WASHINGTON."
#FindWashingtonMissingGirls ...

Missing D.C. Black Girls

Name	Age	Date Last Seen	Area
Jacqueline Lassey	15	Mar 10, 2017	NE
Aniyah McNeil	13	Mar 8, 2017	NW
Dashann Wallace	15	Mar 8, 2017	SE
Yahshaiyah Enoch	13	Mar 8, 2017	SE
Talisha Coles	16	Mar 7, 2017	NE
Morgan Richardson	15	Mar 6, 2017	SE
Dayanna White	15	Mar 3, 2017	SW
Gladys Keitt	18	Mar 2, 2017	SE
Seyauna Parker	14	Feb 24, 2017	NE
Shaquan Scott	15	Feb 16, 2017	SE
Heaven Shamte	15	Feb 2, 2017	SE
Unique Lucas	16	Feb 1, 2017	SE
Chasity Smith	16	Jan 27, 2017	NE

What is God's name is going on further east off I-95 in Washington D.C., where you're having an influx of black and Hispanic missing?

What is happening?

Where is the MEDIA COVERAGE?

I had to go to DC and attempt to learn more, as well as using mi platform on social media, and mi prowess, in such investigatory and research on mi own as much as I can,to study and learn as much insofar as the victims and what happened, and I shall continue to pray hard, do as much as I can to keep the stories of these victims under a spotlight for those who still are awaiting justice. I know how it feel to have a child go missing. March 19 and March 24, nearly a dozen of them black teens aged eleven years young, to age seventeen.(Still missing)at time of books published;

and updated website information @ WOMEN 4 Justice Publishing N.Y.C., and #RedheadBellaMagazineNYC.

Some reports and on social media are citing that at least 13 to 14 hispanic(Latina) and black young children-teens have gone shockingly MISSING within just 24hours.This is beyond outrage, and something more need to be done and keeping MEDIA PRESSURE/SPOTLIGHT on the missing Hispanic black girls,these young children and teen-children will help keep their names front and center at all times until they are FOUND.

Such stories of these missing innocent good souls need to be aggressively investigated. Some feel they are not.

 Chloe Raymond… #HerLifeStillMatters …

Consuelo Ramos-Cruz…#HerLifeStillMatters…

Angela Meade- #HerLifeStillMatters …. So many (As the WASHINGTON DC missing Hispanic, Black good souls who are again reported missing, **sadly** still are remaining as MANY agree about AMBER from LINDEN,NJ that they all remain at the end of the totem pole, it seems, to many when it come down to trying to ascertain what happened."

and where they can feasibly be and if they are still alive and or if foul play is involved, including Jessica Granados.

> These children are still sadly missing in our nation capital and this is just INEXCUSABLE!
>
> Pray for the Washington missing.
>
> Pray they will be found all safe.
>
> Pray they will **SOON**, all be found alive.

There has to be more time devoted everyone, and more available resources as warranted to determine quite simply,

if such developments in such missing cases in Washington, imparticular are an anomaly or is this now becoming as some politicians like Eleanor Homes and others, if this is some type of frightening but reality-trend,but either way we need answers.

We NEED the spotlight around the clock same as when "others"go missing, we need more coverage on BLACK and the HISPANIC sadly gone missing, taken from their loving families, and we **need it now.**

"Whether on Facebook, social media & for years (prior on a site called myspace.com) to now Twitter/FB more and a few other social media sites, more people are using the hashtag #MissingDCGirls **and also are using hashtag demanded aggressive investigation, and stop focusing on the latest so called "rap"video or a 'football basketball jersey" or the next new pair of JORDAN's** you're going to buy today,

 and or other things NOT as relevant as the missing Black and Hispanic missing consistently in Washington; and or are on social media loudly voicing such understable frustration over lack of(severely)devoid of such much needed media coverage in what many believe is an uptick, a serious rise sadly nationwide and statewide, in cases of missing black and hispanic girls, that need to be,and should be receiving:

[SAME AMOUNT OF MEDIA]() TELEVISION COVERAGE REGULAR TV & CABLE NEWS OUTLETS WORLDWIDE,

as other "certain cases"we shall not in the book mention,but many know which cases we are referring to.

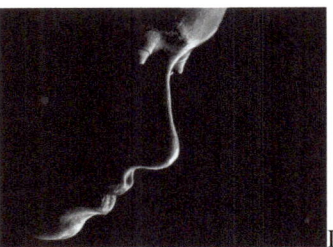 If you're not reporting what you KNOW, then you're part of the problem…From NJ to those murdered/and or missing in Delaware,PA.,to Washington,North Carolina.

#DoTheRightThing as these families deserve to know…

REPORT what you know everyone, tohelp bring these missing children and women, men, back home,where these good souls belong.

Photo(s)all courtesy of Missing Pieces Network; et.al., and seen in the U.S.A.Today recent story during 2017

#SPEAK OUT #REPORT #FINDWashingtonMissingGirls

During April 2017 CNN(unlike FOX news) CNN multi-times have reported on such tragedy taking place. CNN whose covering such story at such time, reported that," Missing Latina girls, Black girls, such crisis is *__an imminent__* crisis for ALL of us.I think most who "care" about these hispanic and black girls gone missing back to back would agree." God bless us all.

BONUS CHAPTER:

"The lost women of North Carolina…"

What in God's name is going on in a quiet nice low-crime rural residential town of Rocky Mount,North Carolina?

The last bonus chapter of this much needed book,is premise all on what has been going on in a town I am fond of, but had no idea about what I am going to share,until I started to research such city,in North Carolina.

I've added this section premise on my beloved parents, always owned properties in FLORIDA, NJ and also own home in nice part(brand new part)community in Rocky Mount. I was a tad-bit befuddled to learn, during mi investigatory going into mi book(s)on unsolved murders, of some of our community citizens,in my tri-state nj/de/pa and ny,and down south in NC., and to learn that feasibly a NC

serial killer (in quiet, nice town of Rocky Mount,)

of multiple BLK women exist right in such town was a surprise.

But not too shocking when we look at such story a bit closer.

This animal,and yes he is an ANIMAL need to be on DEATH ROW.

Not living in a prison cell with phone privilege, and or eating good,breathing,visits etc.al., he deserve DEATH ROW. Anything else for the Rocky Mount serial killer,is not justice.

May the victims all be found,and continue rip(the one's who are confirmed sadly as dead,murdered,

and my heart goes out to the family members left behind,still awaiting their own justice.

I think about these women who were killed,

then found near Seven Bridges Road.

These women(one still not found) have been out there for some time,without the chance to live a full healthy sane blessed by GOD life.

Those who were found near Seven Bridges Rd., had their life snuffed out, by a man who is being called a serial killer,in Rocky Mount,NC.

A town where they are not used of having such crimes darken their nice little rural low-crime town. News reports cite that there were at least five or six women who were all found in the woods right off of Seven Bridges Road,in Northern Edgecombe County.

Two other bodies of these women murdered, not that far away, along with another body found near Scotland Neck.

At one time, only six to seven years ago, NC Governor, during 2010, had immediately issued such emergent call for the NATIONAL GUARD's assistance insofar as trying to find the remaining victims.

At least 90 to 100 National Guardsmen to search.

Such soldiers hail from the 514th military police et.al., and 113nd, for which are headquartered out of respectively, Greenville and also locally in Rocky Mount,NC. Local,federal,state authorities additionally

were searching as well.

The murder of one of the alleged serial killer victims, were named TARAHA SHENICE NICHOLSON.

Reports cite that the only woman(So far) for years now, in which the alleged serial killer was charged with murder, is hers." May she continue to RIP.

If strict law(s)in our beautiful country of U.S.A.,were visible, this would not be happening. In another astute country most recent, a man was found GUILTY by a jury.

He was given a DEATH SENTENCE, rightfully so.

His crime?

Rape of a child under 18 years old.

Murdered her. Abuse of the corpse et.al.,

His punishment?

A PUBLIC HANGING/SHOT DEAD.

He did not have the "soft prison justice we call it" by being able to "meet others" while in prison; have good food any longer,be able to 1 day feasibly be "free"and or live in prison for life,til'he die. That country did it right, as the police cite**, "We shall not tolerate this in our communities." This shall make a criminal think 'twice'** about RAPE. Such man would think twice about taking a gun out and shooting, murder of a innocent or any human being."His hanging was public and shot dead,for what he had done to this poor child.

If America laws were analogous, this would not be happening, and until then, sadly the killing and or the kidnapping of innocent women and children and others will continue.These men do not fear going to prison,since the laws are clearly not tough enough as in other countries.

CONGRESS has the POWER to toughen our laws, to deter, so write to your congress/speak out/take ACTION.

Even though mi tears continue to flow each time I see her pix as well as other victims, I fight mi tears, and remain a staunch 24hrs. a day advocate, and taken ACTION activist, relating to her case being hopefully solved, finally and more media attention to be given on Amber Duncan-Wilson,

my old neighbor's story because she DESERVE it,as all missing children,and murdered children,murdered adults, who should have been able to live a normal happy fun-filled God blessed life,without such innocence and hopes and dreams being swept away.

-

For the Rocky Mount/Edgecombe County NC., alleged serial killer victims(and with his history should have never been out to kill anyone, should've never been allowed in such a beautiful quiet nice community)it is too late.He should not be serving LIFE.

Should not have that privilege.

Take part in our new 21ˢᵗ century POWER-movement for victims of violence, rape,murder,kidnapped/missing children and adults, of color. . . featured in our book(s) and become something yourself,that YOU deep within can be proud of.#TAKEACTION for the victims who can't do it for themselves. #SPEAK OUT #TAKE ACTION

Read more over at:

www.POWERHOUSEWomenMagazine.com

www.WOMEN4JusticePublishingNYC.com

www.RedheadBellaMagazine.com

www.Facebook.com/#TheirLives Still Matter (Remembering AMBER DUNCAN WILSON, Jessica Watson,TOMIENE JONES,Rocky Mount Murder(s) and the Hispanic Black Girls Missing in our Nation's Capital in Washington #TheirLIVESStillMatter featured on FB.

SIGN UP TODAY for update(s)on the AMBER DUNCAN murder, for all new leads, and or to leave tips for law enforcement to bring Amber killer,who has been free for far too long, to JUSTICE as the other killer's of these victims, featured in our book,and also nationwide.

God bless our families…God bless our community and may the murder of AMBER DUNCAN be solved,

and the cheerleader,good student,wonderful human being's murder will not go any longer, UNPUNISHED…

THANKS TO ALL

LAW ENFORCEMENT and ALL VOLUNTEERS et.al.,

WHO ARE APPLYING THE TIME

RESOURCE/EFFORT INSOFAR TO BRING THESE MISSING CHILDREN IN WASHINGTON D.C.,home and in a town the author always respected, and loved,to "find the killer responsible for taking AMBER's life &

for the families in our tri-state NJ-DE-PA.,

& to finally receive, such justice they too deserve...."

GOD BLESS US ALL ...

www.ingramcontent.com/pod-product-compliance
Lightning Source LLC
Chambersburg PA
CBHW041943240526
45473CB00033B/501